1980

ROBERT CREELEY

HELLO:

A JOURNAL, FEBRUARY 29–MAY 3, 1976

A
NEW DIRECTIONS
BOOK

ACKNOWLEDGMENTS
Grateful acknowledgment is made to the editors and publishers of the
following books and magazines, in which some of the material in this book
first appeared: *American Poetry Review, Choice, The Face of Poetry*, La-
Verne H. Clark, ed. (Gallimaufry Press), *Lettera* (Cardiff, Wales), and
Sailing the Road Clear.

Special thanks are due to Alan Loney of the Hawk Press (Christchurch,
New Zealand), who published a limited edition of the New Zealand section
of *Hello* in 1976.

Manufactured in the United States of America
First published clothbound and as New Directions Paperbook 451 in 1978
Published simultaneously in Canada by McClelland & Stewart, Ltd.

Library of Congress Cataloging in Publication Data

Creeley, Robert, 1926–
   Hello: a journal, February 29–May 3, 1976.
   (A New Directions Book)
   I. Title.
PS3505.R43H44   811'.5'4   77-14240
ISBN 0-8112-0674-2
ISBN 0-8112-0675-0 pbk.

New Directions Books are published for James Laughlin
by New Directions Publishing Corporation,
333 Sixth Avenue, New York 10014

for Pen

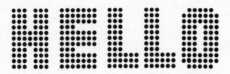

"That's the way
(that's the way

I like it
(I like it"

•

Clouds coming close.

•

Never forget
clouds dawn's
pink red acid
gash—!

•

Here comes
one now!

•

Step out into
space. Good
morning.

•

Well, sleep,
man.

•

Not *man,*
mum's
the word.

•

What do you
think those hills
are going to do now?

•

They got
all the
lights on—
all the people.

•

You know
if you never
you won't

2/29

It's the scale
that's attractive,
and the water
that's around it.

•

Did the young
couple come
only home
from London?

Where's the world
one wants.

•

Singular,
singular,

one
by one.

•

I wish I
could see the stars.

•

Trees *want*
to be still?
Winds
won't let them?

•

Anyhow,
it's night now.

Same clock ticks
in these different places.

3/1

River wandering down
below in the widening green
fields between the hills—
and the sea and the town.

Time settled, or waiting,
or about to be. People,
the old couple, the two babies,
beside me—the so-called

aeroplane. Now
be born,
be born.

                    •

I'll never
see you,
want you,
have you,
know you—

I'll never.

                    •

"Somebody's got to pay
for the squeaks in the bed."

                    •

Such quiet,
dog's scratch at door—

4

pay for it all?

•

Walking
and talking.

Thinking
and drinking.

•

Night.
Light's out.

3/3

"Summa wancha

out back"

Australia

•

"Sonny Terry,
"Brownie McGhee"

in Dunedin (in
Dunedin

3/4

10:30 AM: RALPH HOTERE'S

Warm.
See sun shine.
Look across valley at houses.
Chickens squawk.
Bright glint off roofs.
Water's also,
in bay, in distance.
Hills.

3/5

CHRISTCHURCH

You didn't think you
could do it but you did.

You didn't do it
but you did.

•

CATCHING COLD

I want to lay down
and die—
someday—but
not now.

•

South, north, east, west,
man—home's best.

•

Nary an exit
in Christchurch.

Only
wee holes.

3/9

OUT WINDOW: TAYLOR'S MISTAKE

Silver,
lifting
light—

mist's
faintness.

•

FRIEND SAYS OF JOB

for Barry Southam

You get to see all kinds of life
like man chasing wife
in the driveway
with their car.

Mutual property!
They want to sell their house?

•

Elsewise absences,
eyes a grey blue,
tawny Austrian

hair—the voice,
speaking, *there*.

•

Hermione, in the garden,
"weeping at grief?"

Stone-statued single woman—
eyes alive.

•

MILTON ÜBER ALLES

When I consider
how my life is spent
ere half my years
on this vast blast

are o'er . . .

•

Reasoned recognitions—
feelings fine.

•

Welcome
to the world,
it's still
pretty much the same.

That kiwi
on yon roof
is a symbol,
but the ocean

8

don't change.
It's all *round!*
Don't
let them kid you.

3/11

PALMERSTON NORTH

SOUP

I know what you'd say
if I could ask you—
but I'm tired of it—
no word, nothing again.

Letter from guy says,
"she looks well,
happy, working hard—"
Forget it.

I'm not there.
I'm really here,
sitting,
with my hat on.

It's a great day
in New Zealand
more or less.
I'm not alone in this.

9

Lady out window hangs clothes,
reds and blues—
basket, small kid,
clothespins in mouth.

Do I want to fuck,
or eat?
No problem.
There's a telephone.

I know what you mean,
now "down under" here,
that each life's
got its own condition

to find,
to get on with.
I suppose it's
letting go, finally,

that spooks me.
And of course my arms
are full as usual.
I'm the only one I know.

May I let this be
West Acton, and
myself six? No,
I don't travel that way

despite memories,
all the dear or awful
passages apparently
I've gone through.

Back to the weather,
and dripping nose
I truly wanted to forget here,
but haven't—

ok, old buddy,
no projections, no regrets.
You've been a dear friend
to me in my time.

If it's New Zealand
where it ends,
that makes a weird sense
too. I'd never have guessed it.

Say that all the ways
are one—*consumatum est*—
like some soup
I'd love to eat with you.

3/16

This wide, shallow bowl,
the sun, earth here
moving easy, slow
in the fall, the air
with its lightness, the
underchill now—flat, far out,
to the mountains and the forest.
Come home to its song?

•

Sitting at table—
good talk
with good people.

.

River's glint, wandering
path of it.

Old trees grown tall,
maintain,
look down on it all.

.

Bye-bye, kid says,
girl, about five—
peering look,
digs my one eye.

.

Sun again, on table,
smoke shaft of cigarette,
ticking watch,
chirr of cicadas—
all world, all mind, all heart.

3/17

WELLINGTON

Here again,
shifting days,

on the street.
The people of my life

faded,
last night's dreams,

echoes now.
The vivid sky, blue,

sitting here in the sun—
could I let it go?

Useless question?
Getting old?

    •

I want to be a dog,
when I die—

a dog, a dog.

    •

BRUCE & LINLEY'S HOUSE

Fire back of grate
in charming stove
sits in the chimney hole,
cherry red—
but orange too.

    •

Mrs. Manhire saw me
on plane to Dunedin,
but was too shy to speak
in her lovely Scots accent.

We meet later,
and she notes the sounds are
not very sweet
in sad old Glasgow.

But my wee toughness,
likewise particularity,
nonetheless come
by blood from that city.

.

LOVE

Will you be dust,
reading this?

Will you be sad
when I'm gone.

3/19

SIT DOWN

Behind things
or in front of them,
always a goddamn
adamant number stands

up and shouts,
I'm here, I'm here!
—Sit down.

.

Mother and son
get up,
sit down.

•

NIGHT

Born and bred
in Wellington
she said—

Light high,
street black,
singing still,

"Born & bred
in Wellington,
she said—"

•

DOGGIE BAGS

Don't take
the steak
I ain't
Dunedin

•

The dishes
to the sink
if you've
Dunedin

•

Nowhere
else to go
no I'm not
Dunedin

    •

Ever if
again home
no roam
(at the inn)

Dunedin

    •

MAYBE

Maybe
this way again

someday—
thinking, last night,

of Tim Hardin, girl singing,
"Let me be your rainy day man . . ."

What's the time, dear.
What's happening.

    •

Stay

in Dunedin

for

forever

and a day.

•

Thinking light,
whitish blue,
sun's
shadow on
the porch
floor.

•

Why, in Wellington,
all the "Dunedin"—

Why here
there.

3/21

HAMILTON

HAMILTON HOTEL

Magnolia tree out window
here in Hamilton—
years and years ago
the house, in France,

17

called *Pavillion des Magnolias,*
where we lived and Charlotte
was born, and time's gone
so fast—.

                    •

Singing undersounds,
birds, cicadas—
overcast grey day.

Lady far off across river,
sitting on bench there,
crossed legs, alone.

                    •

If the world's one's
own experience of it,

then why walk around
in it, or think of it.

More would be more
than one could know

alone, more than myself's
small senses, of it.

                3/22

SO THERE

for Penelope

Da. Da. Da da.
Where is the song.
What's wrong
with life

ever. More?
Or less—
days, nights,
these

days. *What's gone*
is gone forever
every time, old friend's
voice here. I want

to stay, somehow,
if I could—
if I would? Where else
to go.

The sea here's out
the window, old
switcher's house, vertical,
railroad blues, *lonesome*

whistle, etc. Can you
think of Yee's Cafe
in Needles, California
opposite the train

station—can you keep
it ever
together, old buddy, talking
to yourself again?

Meantime some *yuk*
in Hamilton has blown
the whistle on a charming
evening I wanted

to remember otherwise—
the river there, that
afternoon, sitting,
friends, wine & chicken,

watching the world go by.
Happiness, happiness—
so simple. What's
that anger is that

competition—sad!—
when this at least
is free,
to put it mildly.

My aunt Bernice
in Nokomis,
Florida's last act,
a poem for Geo. Washington's

birthday. Do you want
to say "it's bad"?
In America, old sport,
we shoot first, talk later,

or just take you out to dinner.
No worries, or not
at the moment,
sitting here eating bread,

cheese, butter, white wine—
like Bolinas, "Whale Town,"
my home, like they say,
in America. It's *one* world,

it can't be another.
So the beauty,
beside me, rises,
looks now out window—

and breath keeps on breathing,
heart's pulled in
a sudden deep, sad
longing, to want

to stay—be another
person some day,
when I grow up.
The world's somehow

forever that way
and its lovely, roily,
shifting shores, sounding now,
in my ears. My ears?

Well, what's on my head
as two skin appendages,
comes with the package.
I don't want to

argue the point.
Tomorrow
it changes, gone,
abstract, new places—

moving on. Is this
some old time weird
Odysseus trip
sans paddle—up

the endless creek?
Thinking of you,
baby, thinking
of all the things

I'd like to say and do.
Old fashioned time
it takes to be
anywhere, at all.

Moving on. Mr. Ocean,
Mr. Sky's
got the biggest blue eyes
in creation—

here comes the sun!
While we can,
let's do it, let's
have fun.

3/26

NOW

Hard to believe
it's all *me*

whatever
this world

of space & time,
this place,

body,
white,

inutile,
fumbling at the mirror.

3/27

YAH

Sure I fell in love—
"with a very lovely person."
You'd love her too.
"She's lovely."

•

Funny what your head
does, waking up

in room, world,
you never saw before,

each night new.
Beautiful view, like they say,

this time, Sydney—
whose always been a friend of mine.

Boats out there, dig it?
Trees so green you could

eat them, grass too.
People, by god—

"so you finally got here?"
Yeah, passing through.

 •

One person
and a dog.

 •

Woman staggering
center of street—

wop!
Messy.

All in
the mind.

 •

Long
legged
dark
man

I think.

.

Hey Cheryl!
Talk

to me.
Yiss?

Say it like this.

.

I love
Australia—

it's so big
and fuzzy

in bed.

.

THEN

Don't go
to the mountains,

again—not
away, mad. Let's

talk it out, you
never went anywhere.

I did—and here
in the world, looking back

on so-called life
with its impeccable

talk and legs and breasts,
I loved you

but not as some
gross habit, please.

Your voice
so quiet now,

so vacant, for me,
no sound, on the phone,

no clothes, on the floor,
no face, no hands,

—if I didn't want
to be here, I wouldn't

be here, and would
be elsewhere? Then.

3/28

WINDOW

Aching sense
of being

person—body in-
side, out—

the houses, sky,
the colors, sounds.

3/29

PLACES

All but
for me and Paul.

.

Off
of.

3/30

EN ROUTE PERTH

FOR CHERYL

Sitting here in limbo, "there are
sixteen different shades of red."

27

Sitting here in limbo, there are
people walking through my head.

If I thought I'd think it different,
I'd just be dumber than I said.

•

Hearing sounds in
plane's landing gear lowering:

I don' wanna

3/31

SINGAPORE

MEN

Here, on the wall
of this hotel in
Singapore, there's a

picture, of a woman,
big-breasted, walking,
blue-coated, with

smaller person—both
followed by a house men
are carrying. It's a day

in the life of the world.
It tells you, somehow,
what you ought to know.

•

Getting fainter, in the world,
fearing something's fading,
deadened, tentative responses—
go hours without eating,
scared without someone to be
with me. These empty days.

•

Growth, trees, out window's
reminiscent of other days,

other places, years ago,
a kid in Burma, war,

fascinated, in jungle,
happily not shot at,

hauling the dead and dying
along those impossible roads

to nothing much could help.
Dreaming, of home, the girl

left behind, getting drunk,
getting laid, getting beaten

out of whorehouse one night.
So where am I now.

•

Patience gets
you the next place.

So they say.

•

Some huge clock
somewhere said it was
something like sixteen

or twenty hours later
or earlier there, going
around and around.

•

BLUE RABBIT

Things going quiet
got other things

in mind. That rabbit's
scared of me! I can't

drag it out by the ears
again just to look.

•

I'll remember the dog,
with the varicolored,

painted head, sat
beside me, in Perth,

while I was talking
to the people

in the classroom—
and seemed to listen.

4/4

COUNTRY WESTERN

Faint dusky light
at sunset—park,

Manila—people
flooding the flatness,
speakers, music:

"Yet I did

"the best I could

"with what I had . . ."

•

HERE AGAIN

No sadness
in the many—
only the one,
separate, looks
to see another
come. So it's

all by myself
again, one
way or another.

•

LATER

Later than any time
can tell me, finding
ways now as I can—

any blame, anything
I shouldn't do, any
thing forgotten, any way

to continue, this little
way, these smaller ways—
pride I had, what I thought

I could do, had done.
Anyone, anything, still
out there—is there some

one possible, something
not in mind still as
my mind, my way. I

persist only in wanting,
only in thinking, only now
in waiting, for that way

to be the way I can
still let go, still want, and
still let go, and want to.

4/5

MANILA

Life goes on living,
sitting in chair here

in café at Domestic Airport—
heat stirring my skin & bones,

and people like dusty
old movie, Peter Lorre, and

I don't see no criminals
looking at nobody, only

myriad people on this final
island of the ultimate world.

    •

Each time *sick loss*
feeling starts to hit me,
think of *more* than that,
more than "I" thought of.

    •

Early morning still—
"announcing the ah-ri-

val" of world in little,
soft, wet, sticky pieces.

    •

You can tilt the world
by looking at it sideways—

or you can put it up-
side down by standing on

33

your head—and underneath,
or on end, or this way,

or that, the waves come in,
and grass grows.

•

BREAKING UP IS HARD TO DO

"Don't take your love
"away from me—

"Don't leave my heart
"in misery . . ."

I know that it's
true. I know.

•

One day here
seems like years now

since plane came in
from Singapore—

heart in a bucket,
head in hand.

•

Falling to sleep nights
like losing balance—

crash!—wake to bright
sunlight, time to go!

CEBU

Magellan was x'ed here
but not much now left,

seemingly, of that event
but for hotel's name—

and fact of boats filling
the channel. And the churches,

of course, as Mexico, as all of
Central and South America.

Driving in from the airport,
hot, trying to get bearings—

witness easy seeming pace of the place,
banana trees, mangos, the high

vine grapes on their trellises.
But particularly the people moseying

along. Also the detention home
for boys, and another casual prison

beside the old airport now
used for light planes. I saw

in a recent paper a picture
of a triangular highrise in Chicago,

downtown, a new prison there,
looking like a modern hotel.

Also in Singapore there are
many, many new buildings—

crash housing for the poor,
that hurtles them skyward off

the only physical thing they
had left. Wild to see clotheslines,

flapping shirts, pants, dresses,
something like thirty stories up!

I'd choose, no doubt dumbly,
to keep my feet on the ground—

and I like these houses here,
open-sided, thatched roofed—

that could all be gone in a flash,
or molder more slowly

back into humus. One doesn't
finally want it all forever,

not stopped there, in abstract
time. Whatever, it's got to

be yielded, let go of, it can't
live any longer than it has to.

Being human, at times I
get scared, of dying, growing

old, and think my body's
possibly the exception to all

that I know has to happen.
It isn't, and some of those

bananas are already rotten,
and no doubt there are vacant

falling-down houses, and boats
with holes in their bottoms

no one any longer cares about.
That's all right, and I can

dig it, yield to it, let what
world I do have be the world.

In this room the air-conditioner
echoes the southwest of America—

my mother-in-law's, in Albuquerque,
and I wonder what she's doing

today, and if she's happy there,
as I am here, with these green

walls, and the lights on, and
finally loving everything I know.

4/7

MORNING

Dam's broke,
head's a
waterfall.

DAVAO INSULAR HOTEL

You couldn't get it
off here in a million

obvious years, shrubs cut
to make animals, bluish,

reddish, purple lights
illuminating the pool—

and the only lady within
miles to talk to tells me

she got culture-shocked by
multiple single-seat tv sets

in bus stations, airports, in
the States. So we're single

persons, so the jungle's
shrunk to woods, and

38

people are Jim and Mary—
have a drink. I can't

believe the solution's this
place either, three hundred

calculated persons to each
and every family unit,

sucking like mad to get fed.
Extended, distended—no

intent ever to be more or
less than the one sits next

to you, holds your hand,
and, on occasion, fucks.

4/8

BALER

APOCALYPSE NOW

Waiting to see if
Manila's a possi-
bility, yellow plane
of Francis F. Coppalo
on tarmac fifty
yards away—kids,
coins, flipping, air
wet, rather warm—

no movies today,
friends—just sit
in air, on bench, be-
fore cantina, listen
to words of mouths
talking Tagalog,
and "I swear I
love my husband"—
I could spend quite
a bit of time here,
but by nine in
the morning, I hope
I can get home.

·

Wrong: white man's
over-reach, teeth
eating tongue, spoken
beforehand, al-
ready.

4/10

SINGAPORE

EVENING

Walking street back here,
the main drag for the money,
and lights just going on,
day faded, people hot, distracted—

one person, walking, feeling older
now, heavier, from chest to hips
a lump won't move with my legs,
and all of it tireder, slower—

flashes in store windows, person
with somewhat silly hat on,
heavy-waisted, *big*, in the company,
and out of step, out of place—

back to the lone hotel room,
sit here now, writing this,
thinking of the next step,
and when and how to take it.

•

Split mind, hearing voice—
two worlds, two places.

4/11

TALKING

Faded back last night
into older dreams, some

boyhood lost innocences.
The streets have become inaccessible

and when I think of people,
I am somehow not one of them.

Talking to the doctor-
novelist, he read me a poem

of a man's horror, in Vietnam,
child and wife lost to him—

his own son sat across from me,
about eight, thin, intent—

and myself was like a huge,
fading balloon, that could hear

but not be heard, though we
talked and became clear friends.

I wanted to tell him I was
an honest, caring man. I wanted

the world to be more simple,
for all of us. His wife said,

driving back, that my hotel's bar
was a swinging place in the '50s.

It was a dark, fading night.
She spoke quickly, obliquely,

along for the ride, sitting
in the front seat beside him.

I could have disappeared, gone
away, seen them fading too,

war and peace, death,
life, still no one.

•

Why want
to be so *one*
when it's not
enough?

•

Down and
down, over
and out.

4/13

OLD SAYING

There is no
more.

•

Start again
from the beginning then.

4/14

HOTEL LOBBY

Sun out window's
a blessing, air's
warmth and wetness.

43

The people fade,
melt, in the mind.

•

No scale, no congruence,
enough.

•

This must be some
time-stream, persons
all the same.

•

How call back,
or speak forward?

Keep the physical
literal.

•

Play on it,
jump up.

•

I don't
look like
anybody
here!

•

Funny how
people pick
their noses.

•

RIDING WITH SAL

for Salleh

Pounding VW motor
past the people, cars—

hot day in downtown
Kuala Lumpur, and the

Chinese-lunch-style
conversation's still in mind,

"do Americans look *down*
on Asians?" Is the world

round, or flat, is it
one, or two, or many—

and what's a Muslim
like you doing here

anyhow. Breeze lifts,
sun brightens at edges,

trees crouch under
towering hotel's walls.

Go to Afghanistan and
be Sufis together, brother,

dance to *that* old in-
veterate wisdom after all.

•

SUFI SAM CHRISTIAN

Lift me into heaven
slowly 'cause my back's

sore and my mind's too
thoughtful, and I'm not

even sure I want to go.

·

LUNCH AND AFTER

I don't want to leave
so quickly, the lovely

faces, surrounding, human
terms so attractive. And

the world, the *world,* we
could think of, *here,* to-

gether, a flash of instant, a
million years of time.

Don't, myself, be an
old man yet, I want to

move out and into this
physical, endless place.

Sun's dazzling shine now
back of the towering clouds,

and sounds of builders'
pounding, faint, distant

buzz of traffic. Mirror's
in front of me, hat's on

head, under it, human
face, my face, reddened,

it seems, lined, grey's
in beard and mustache—

not only *myself* but an-
other man has got to

at last walk out and into
another existence, out there,

that haze that softens those trees,
all those other days to come.

•

WAR & PEACE

Cannot want not to
want, cannot. Thinks

later, acts
now.

•

HOTEL MERLIN

On the seventeenth
floor of this

modern building, in
room I accepted

gratefully, bed I
lay down on—

vow to think
more responsibly?

Vow to be
kinder to

mother (dead), brothers
(dead), sister—

who loves me?
Will I now see

this world as
possible arrangement.

Will I eat
less, work more

for common ends?
Will I turn from friends,

who are not friends?
Will judgment,

measure
of such order,

rule me?
Or will flash of willful

impulse
still demand

whatever life,
whatever death.

.

SEVENTEENTH FLOOR:
ECHOES OF SINGAPORE

No one's going to
see me naked up here.

My only chance is
to jump.

4/15

UP HERE

Place in mind
or literal, out window,
"too abstract"—

a long way down
to the street—
or home.

.

TIME

Can't live,
mindless,
in present—

can't make past,
or future,
enough place.

4/16

4/16

HONG KONG

REMEMBER

Sweltering, close
dreams of a
possible heaven—

before sleeping mind,
before waking
up to dead day.

•

HONG KONG WINDOW

Seemingly awash
in this
place, *here*—

egocentric
abstraction—
no one

else but
me again,
and people,

people as if
behind glass,
close

but untouchable.
What
was the world

I'd thought of,
who
was to be there?

The buildings
lean in
this window,

hotel's abstraction,
cars
like toys pass,

below,
fourteen stories
down

on those streets.
In park
kids wade

in a pool.
Grey day,
in spring,

waits for rain.
"What's
the question?"

Who asks it,
which *me*
of what life.

      •

PARK

Like in the Brownie Books—
people below, in distance,
like little moving dots of color,
look at 'em go!

      •

Buildings against hillsides
waiting for night
to make a move.

      •

Something about the vertical
and the horizontal
out of whack possibly,

viz., the buildings
look like they could walk,
and in the flat park,

below, the people are
walking, and running even,
but I can't put the two together.

      •

SIGN

"SIEMENS" not
semen's, and I don't
see men's—and I don't
know what it means.

·

BUILDINGS

Why not make them
higher, and higher, and
higher—until they fall down?

·

Something about raw side
of cut cliff, with building
jammed against it, still hurts.

·

With world now
four billion, you
haven't even started yet.

·

Sentimental
about earth
and water,

and people?
Still got enough
to share?

·

But if you don't,
you won't
have it long.

•

The money's singing
in the walls of this building.

•

Sun's out. Big
lazy clouds float
over the buildings.
Thank god.

•

PARK

Why did that man
fly the kid's kite
precisely into the trees

when a wide space
of bare ground was
a few feet away. Was it

the women, with them,
sitting on the park bench,
didn't want to move.

•

Kid's face, lifting
big yellow speed boat
with proper gas motor

out of pool after
it's conked out, all
the other kids around,

watching him. He's in
some sad defensive place
now. It's still his.

•

Lots of older
women here talking
to younger women.

Now one, by herself,
pregnant, walks by.
Her legs look thin from the back.

•

This park is really used.
It's got bare ground
like in Boston.

•

Can see tennis players,
with roller skaters behind them.
"One world."

•

Trees dancing now.
They dig it.

•

And you can't
be alone for long.

4/19

HONG KONG—LAST WORDS

I want to get off
the fucking world and
sit down in a chair,
and be there.

4/21

THINGS TO DO IN TOKYO

for Ted Berrigan

Wake up.
Go to sleep.
Sit *zazen* five days
in five minutes.

Talk
to the beauty next to me
on plane, go-
ing to San Francisco.

Think it's all a dream.
Return
"passport, wallet and ticket"
to man I'd taken them from.

No mistakes.
This time.
Remember mother
ashed in an instant.

No tears.
No way, other than this one.
Wander. Sing
songs from memory. Tell

classical Chinese poet
Bob Dylan's the same.
Sit again in air.
Be American.

Love. Eat
Unspeakable Chicken—
"old in vain."
Lettuce, tomato—

bread. Be humble.
Think again.
Remy Martin is
Pete Martin's brother?

Drink. Think
of meeting Richard Brautigan,
and brandy, years ago.
(All the wonder,

all the splendor,
of Ezra Pound!)
Don't be dismayed,
don't be cheap.

No Hong Kong,
no nothing.
Be on the way
to the way

to the way.
Every day's happy,
sad. "That's the way"
to think. Love

people, all over.
Begin at the beginning,
find the end.
Remember everything,

forget it. Go on,
and on. Find ecstasy,
forget it.
Eat chicken entirely,

recall absent friends.
Love wife
by yourself, love
women, men,

children.
Drink, eat
"and be merry." Sleep
when you can. Dogs

possibly human?—
not cats or birds.
Let all openings be openings.
Simple holes.

Virtue is people,
mind's eye in trees,
sky above,
below's water, earth.

Keep the beat
Confucian—"who
controls." Think man's
possibly beauty's brother,

or husband.
No matter, no mind.
It's here, it's around.
Sing

deliberately.
Love all relations,
be father to daughters,
sons. Respect

wife's previous residence
in Tokyo, stories
she told. All time,
all mind, all

worlds,
can't exist
by definition—
are one.

•

THE WINNER

I'm going to beat
everything I can.

•

AMERICAN LOVE

A big assed
beauty!

•

MEMORY

A fresh
sea breeze.

•

THE

[Thinking of L.Z., "That one
could, etc."]

A's

4/21

KYOTO

INN/KYOTO

Suddenly *here,*
let down, into room,
as if bare—

tea,
and packaged small cake,
food also for thought—

squat
on bottom, floor,
feel heavy—

but sure of place,
in place.
Where time's been,

years, a humor
can't
be absent.

So woman, my age,
who's led me
through corridor,

slides door open,
comes into room again,
laughs

at misunderstanding.
"The bath
tonight?" No,

tomorrow
night. "Eat
Japanese

in the morning?"
Eat—
in the morning.

4/23

FOR BENNY

Kids of Kyoto
visible through split
bamboo screen—

across canal
to street. One lifts
her skirt, blue,

to reveal red underpants
her friend
then examines.

It's a small world,
these subtle
wooden houses,

sliding screens,
mats on floor,
water running

so often within hearing—
all that, and the
keeper of this tiny inn,

a woman, laughs,
thank god, as I crash
from wall to wall.

I'm sitting here,
having seen six
temples this morning,

wondering if I lack
religion. Old man
now passes,

shaved head, grey clothes,
and a woman stops
to look in her purse.

It's just about
four o'clock—
it's grey, shifting clouds,

no rain as yet.
I like it, and I'm happy
to sleep on the floor,

which I do, like a log.
It's truly time
to study the water,

passing, each specific
ripple, flicker
of light—take

everything I know
and put it out there,
where it's got to go.

4/24

LATER

Drunks leaning on your arm,
and the endless drinking
in Japan, and going
to Osaka—

"where the men chew tobacker
and the women wiggy-
waggy-woo . . ."

•

No way
today.

•

CHEAP THRILL

Write in air
with flourishes.

4/25

WOMEN

I'll always
look that way
to see
where I'm going.

4/27

64

SEOUL SOUNDS

for English Literary Society
of Korea

Weird, flat seeming—
tho' mountains surround—
old Seoul!

And they's got
soul-food
and soul-folk, these

instant Irish.
Syncretic,
someone said, when

I'd asked, was there
Confucian true root?
Much mixed in,

thus, but tough,
hold to it,
push back.

Sentimental,
like Americans—
cry and laugh!

Once in, confusions
grow less,
though day's grey

and I'm stretched,
got to talk
in an hour.

But here
in this room, there's
a peace, and some hope

I can say it,
make words sing
human truth:

If one's still
of *many,*
then one's not alone—

If one lives
with *people,*
then one has a home.

•

PLACE

for Maria

Let's take
any
of the information of

this world and
make a picture,
dig. The

fact of things,
you know, the
edges, pieces

of so-called
reality, will doubtless
surface. So

surfaces—abstract
initial e-
vent—are—

god knows, god
possibly cares, and
now some *other*

"thing" is
the case, viz., "I
love you," now
I'm here.

4/29

MARIA SPEAKS

Still morning
again. "Mendel's
successor—" the

Zen brother
next door
who kept

insects in
a jar—perfected
listening

to things
"spreading their legs,"
"fish tanks filled with bugs."

•

KIDS/SEOUL

Watching incredible kids
cross street, against traffic,
pushing a bike—

little girl leads, hand
on the handlebars—
heart's so content

to be pleased,
to find joy,
like they say,

can be simple.

•

TALK

Talking Ginsbergian
chop-talk's
a pleasure—see

person, find face
right over middle.
Look down for shoes,

legs just above.
Something to look at,
and something to love!

4/30

THERE

Miles back
in the wake,
days faded—

nights sleep seemed
falling down
into some deadness—

killing it,
thinking dullness,
thinking body

was dying.
Then
you changed it.

.

CLOCK

How to live
with some plan
puts the days

into emptiness,
fills time
with time?

.

Not much
left to go on—
it's moving
out.

●

GIFTS

Giving me things,
weights accumulate.

I wish
you wouldn't—

I wish we
could eat

somewhere,
drink.

●

FRIEND

"Father's dead,"
feel flutter,

wings, trying
to beat the dark.

●

GOING HOME

You'll love me
later, after

you've tried
everything else

and got tired.
But body's

catching up,
time's lost

as possibility.
Mind's no longer

a way
tonight.

5/1

SEOUL

Korean slang
for Americans:

"hellos"

·

9:45 AM
Sitting in plane still
in airport, bright

tight sunlight
thru window, guy

sitting in seat alongside,
Japanese, flips pages

of white book. In the aisle
people wander, looking for seats.

            •

Nobody here to love
enough to want to.

            •

American chichi traveler
just flashed past, her
long brown hair wide open!

            •

Catches pillow
flipped to her—

In charge.

            •

PROBABLE TRUTH

It's best
to die
when you can.

PLACE

Long gone time—
waves still crash in?
Fall coming on?

.

Shifting head to
make transition, rapid
mind to think it.

.

Halfway to wherever,
places, things
I used to do.

.

OUT HERE

People having a good time
in the duty free shop,
Tokyo Airport—

can you knock it. Recall
Irving Layton's classic line
re his mother: "her face

was flushed with bargains, etc."
Can't finally think
the world is good guys

and bad guys, tho' these creeps
drive me back into this
corner of the bar—but I'd

choose it anyhow, sit,
hoping for company. A few
minutes ago I was thinking:

"Fuck me, Ruby, right
between the eyes!"
Not any more, it's later,

and is going to get later yet
'fore I get on plane, go home,
go somewhere else at least.

It's raining, outside, in
this interjurisdictional headquarters.
I'm spooked, tired, and approaching

my fiftieth birthday. Appropriately
I feel happy, and sad,
at the same time. I think of

Peter Warshall's amulet I've worn
round my neck for two months now—
turtle, with blue bead cosmos—

that's enough. Nancy Whitefield's
childhood St. Christopher's medal
has stayed safe in the little box

wherein I keep fingernail clippers,
and a collar button, and several
small stones I picked up on a beach.

People still around but
they're fading out now to
get another plane. Hostess,

picking up her several fried chicken
quick lunches, smiles at me,
going past. Guy with spoonbill

blue cap and apparently
American bicentennial mottoes
on front of it, orders a San Miguel

beer. Now he knocks on glass door,
adjacent, I guess his wife's on
the other side. Days, days

and nights, and more of same—
and who wins, loses, never
that simple to figure out.

I'll be a long way away
when you read this—and I won't
remember what I said.

.

DEAR

You're getting fat,
dear.

.

THEN

Put yourself where you'll be
in five hours
and look back

and see if you'd do the same
the way you're doing it
all the time.

•

That's not easy
to think about.

•

It was
once.

•

WHICH IS TO SAY

You could do everything
you could do.

•

Killing time
by not looking
by killing time.

•

JAWS

See one more person
chewing something
I'll eat them both.

•

Kid's giggling
obbligato.

•

No one's going
anywhere.

•

EPIC

Save some room
for my epic.

•

Absence makes
a hole.

•

Any story
begins somewhere

and any other story
begins somewhere else.

•

HERE

Since I can't
kill anyone,
I'd better
sit still.

•

SHE'S BACK!

Styles of drinking, the cool
hand extended, the woman
with the one leg crossed,

sticking out. Now the handsome
one walks off, business
completed. Time to go.

•

If you could look
as good as you could
look, you surely would.

•

EYES

Tall
dark
woman

with
black, wide,
shadowed eyes.

•

Great
shade of orange.

•

I don't do this
for nothing yet.

•

Hours
pass.

·

HERE
Sounds like ball
in bowling alley.

Music's
underneath it.

Clapped
hands.

Hums
of various conversations,

people sitting out
on couches,

wide,
low ceilinged space.

Kimonoed kid
sits on floor with buddy.

·

Three.
Straight up.

·

Each one
trying to stay someone.

79

SAY SOMETHING

Say something
to me. "Could you
help me with
this . . ." Such

possibly the woman's
(Thailand) speech
in aisle adjacent,
plane's body, going

through night. It's
going home, with me—
months passed,
things happened in.

I need some
summary, gloss
of it all, days
later. Last recall

was Bobbie in
the kitchen saying
apropos coat, "If
you don't wear it

now, you never will . . ."
Or Bobbie, at airport.
re people—
"They all look

like R. Crumb
characters . . ." It
drifts, it
stays by itself.

•

Friends I've loved
all the time,
Joanne,
Shao—but

not so
simply
now
to name them.

•

I could get drunker
and wiser
and lower
and higher.

•

Peter's
amulet
worked!

•

KYOTO

"Arthur's friend's
a nice man!"

•

MEMORY

Nancy finally
at the kitchen table.

·

BOBBIE

Her voice,
her voice, her
lovely voice . . .

·

Now's
the time.

·

Watching water
blast up
on window
Provincetown—

clouds, air, trees,
ground,
watching for
the next one.

·

One's so neat
about it.

·

ECHO

Faint, persistent
smell of shit.

•

MOMMY

Kid's been crying
so long.

•

IF YOU'RE GOING TO HAVE ONE

The Chinese, Koreans,
Filipinos, persons from
Thailand

"are better fathers and mothers."

•

ON BOARD

The mommy,
daddy

number.

•

God a
crying
kid.

•

LATER

It feels things
are muddled again
when I wanted
my head straight—

in this empty place,
people sleeping, light
from another person
reading lets me see.

That's talking about it.
This is—this is
where I've been before
and now don't want to go back to.

•

No blaming anyone,
nothing I can't do,
nowhere to be happy
but where I am.

•

Plans—the next
six months
all arranged.

•

You can see her face,
hear her voice,
hope it's happy.

5/3

A NOTE

To move in such fashion through nine countries (Fiji was my first stop, so to speak) in a little over two months is a peculiarly American circumstance, and the record thus provoked is *personal* in a manner not only the effect of my own egocentricity, but, again, a fact of American social reality. The tourist will always be singular, no matter what the occasion otherwise—and there is a sense, I think, in which Americans still presume the world as something to look at and use, rather than to live in. Again and again, I found that other cultural patterns, be they Samoan, Chinese, Malaysian, or Filipino, could not easily think of one as singular, and such familiar concepts as the "nuclear family" or "alienation" had literally to be translated for them. Whereas our habit of social value constantly promotes an isolation—the house in the country, the children in good schools— theirs, of necessity, finds center and strength in the collective, unless it has been perverted by Western exploitation and greed.

Not long ago, reading poems at a communal center in Indianapolis, I was asked by a member of the black community to explain my going to such places as the Philippines and South Korea—where overtly fascist governments are in power—sponsored by our State Department. The same question was put to me by an old friend indeed, Cid Corman, in Kyoto. How could I answer? That I am American? That the government is mine too? I wish I might find so simply a vindication. No, I went because I wanted to—to look, to see, even so briefly, how people in those parts of the world made a reality, to talk of being American, of the past war, of power, of usual life in this country, of my fellow and sister poets, of my neighbors on Fargo Street in Buffalo, New York. I wanted, at last, to be *human,* however simplistic that wish. I took thus my own chances, and remarkably found a company. My deepest thanks to them all.

—R.C.